With Stars in Her Eyes

A collection of poetry

Written by Karalyn Elyse
Illustrated by Carys Rae

Book Cover by Karalyn Elyse & Carys Rae

Illustrations by Carys Rae

Publishd by The Nights & Weekends

1st edition 2026

For Deb
I miss you, friend. Thank you for praying for me.

&

For Eden-bean & Sol
May God bless you and protect you. May He make His face shine on you and be gracious to you. May He look on you with favor and give you peace.

Introduction

If you are reading this and have read my previous collection, *The Idle Lighthouse*, I think I should tell you right now that this collection will be very different. This collection is a compilation of poetry written over a handful of years that depicts a journey of self. It might end up being the collection I am most afraid to share, because it is the most vulnerable and raw.

The collection is split up into three parts; Was, Am, and Becoming. While the poems were not written completely in chronological order (I wrote "He is still giving me better things" back in my college days), they do each correlate with the highs and lows of my mental, emotional and spiritual states. Many of my "Was" poems were written during some of the lowest moments of my life, and "Becoming" written at some of the highest.

Life is full of emotions, and for a long time, I neglected mine. I thought that feeling sorrow and grief were too much—too hard. So I turned away from them, and in doing so, also turned from feeling the heights of joy and peace. I am eternally grateful for the friends who urged me to allow myself to feel, truly feel, all of my emotions, and to the Grace that was given to me to have the opportunity to change.

If you have read this far, thank you. Truly, thank you. The poems that you will soon read are glimpses into a broken person, redeemed by no work of their own. There will be poems that tackle the fractured fear of being broken, and poems that tightly grip the fringes of grace and hope. My story is still unfolding, my journey still underway, but I am ready to part with these poems by sharing them with those who would choose to pick up this little book. I hope you, dear reader, see the hope that there is in the process, in the waiting, and in the redeeming.

Content

Part I: Was

"why can't i sleep at night?

Knotted stomach and
Shallow breath.
Narrow focus and pushing back at
Fear.
Anxiety.
Overwhelming-ness.
I am t
u
r
b
u
l
e
n
t

“abyss”

There is this
dark abyss
that opens its mouth
every once
in a while.
It is there,
don’t you see it?
Right behind me,
ever present.
I try my best
to ignore,
the gnawing feeling
that I will never
escape.
That if I look,
I will fall,
down
down
down
and never
get out
again.

“psyche of my inner monologue”

Undeserved thoughts
have wrought
havoc and chaos
on the psyche of
my inner monologue.

I’m aware I’m not
together, not
the same.
I’ve experienced trauma.
I’ve felt shame.

The disarray
has betrayed the
picture perfect life
I paint
on the canvas of
my brain.

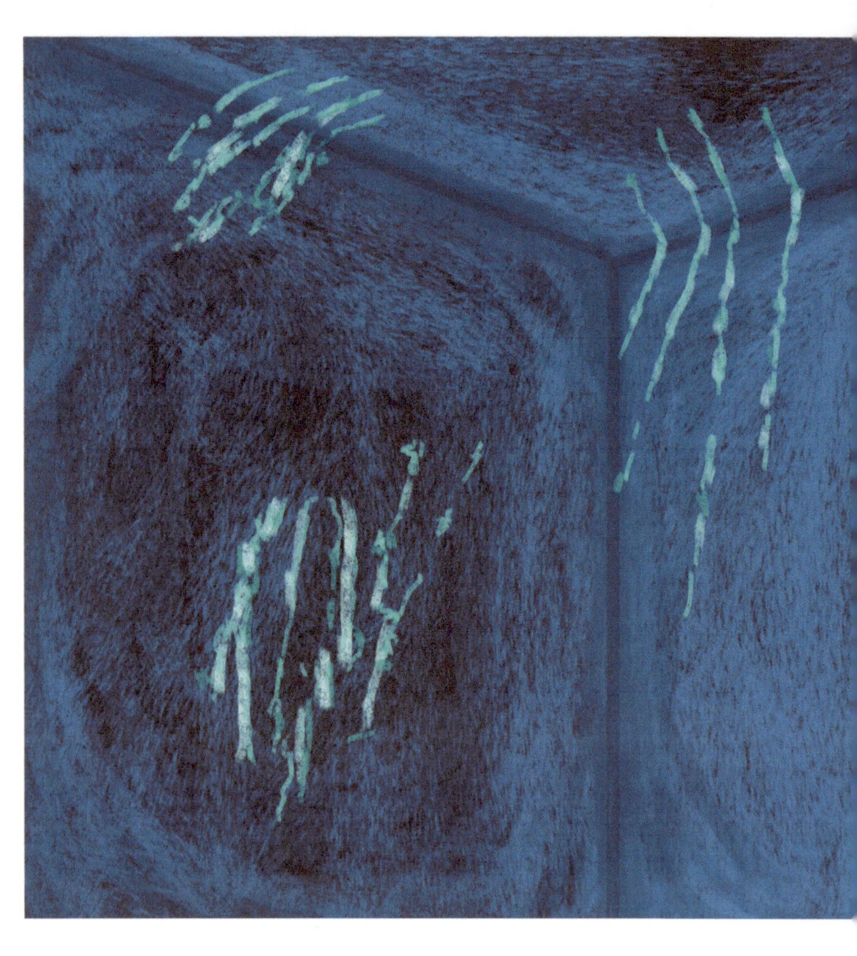

“go”

Used.
I
am
weary for rest
and
Peace.

Change
from
this
box I’ve been
pushed
into.

I need
to
Go.

“acrostic”

Bravely I tread
Across
Roads and
Ruins I once
Enjoyed but
Now find only dismay.

“please, see love bloom again”

It is hard
to not be bitter
and sad.
I see love
bloom and grow
and then leave.

Love has eluded me
time and time again.
So those who find
the mate they choose
for their soul
should hold fast.
Weather the winter
and see love bloom again.

"my wild heart"

My wild heart
has no bounds.
It gulps adventure down
like fresh air.

I'm a child again,
but older. Wiser.
I'm dreaming again.
hoping again.

I am trusting
love one more time.
and another.
and another.

Maybe one day
I will understand.
look back
and see the plan.

But for now
I trust.
Again and again
and again.

"soft again"

I hope
to always be soft.
I want to be kind
for others.
I have been
callous for
much too long and I
wish to be soft
again.

“old friend”

I love
the ocean.

After all this time,
it still
knows
me.

“this doesn’t feel right”

I always thought
growing up
meant growing more but
it feels more
like growing farther
and farther
behind.

“weary”

Untethered.
Adrift.
My heart
is lost
among the tumultuous sea.

Adrift.
Untethered.
As hope dims
and my soul
yearns for rest.
Reprieve.

This life
full of want
wearies me.

"cycle thoughts"

You're not enough.
You're too much.
You are annoying.
You aren't funny.
You're flaky.
You're of no consequence.
You're not smart enough.
You are arrogant.
You're not confident enough.
You are full of yourself.
You're a pushover.
You're rude.
You are too emotional.
You're distant & cold.
You're inconsistent.
You're undesirable.
You are immature.
You are overwhelming.
You are ungrateful.
You are ridiculous.
You are an air-head.
You talk too much.
You are too quiet.
You won't be accepted.
You're nothing special.
You're unloved.
You're too weird.

"hardened heart"

Not allowed.
Those thoughts, potential
to feel—no.

I will guard this wall.
It was I
who built it and
I will tend it.

The creeping ivy
is an unnecessary companion.
I trim and cut
but it keeps
coming
back.

“never going back”

It’s not hard
to lose oneself.
In fact,
it happens slowly.
Sometimes it happens
with your permission.

I lost myself
and gladly did so.
I lost color.
I lost beauty.
But I had no
trust to lose.

And then
I found myself.
I found the
young girl who
believed in magic
and true love.
And I hope
never to lose
her again.

Part II: Am

“the fog is lifting”

Expectation turns to
gathering ruffled hope.

Strung together and fisted tightly,
I cling to dreams and
cherished yearnings.

"it's been a while"

Friendships rekindle and
the story resumes—
it's pause
but a breath.

Blessings not asked for
as hope returns.

“expectations”

The dreams
of my youth
I often confuse
with promises
not given.
All I have
is now,
and eternity.

“presence”

Before the Sun,
before the thoughts,
I tread along the shore.

That stilling quiet,
the embrace of nearness,
wraps around me.

And as Day makes
her exquisite entrance,
I am not alone.

“in awe”

Boisterous laughter
echoes in the chambers
of my soul.

Joy, found in
unseen things.
In unearned marvels.

"was i ever going to be enough?"

When did I
become less than
to you
because I lack a
man, spouse, child?

Was it 23?
Was it 25?
Because I
feel it keenly
at 27.

"high standards"

Eldest daughter obligations.
Mature and marry,
bear and brave,
carry and care.

Church kid expectations
of marriage and family
pester me year after year.

The pressure is mounting.
I won't give in—
not for just anyone.

Because I want both
adventure and home,
thrills and peace,
love and freedom.

I've waited my whole life.
I can wait longer.
Because I will not settle—
I will not compromise.

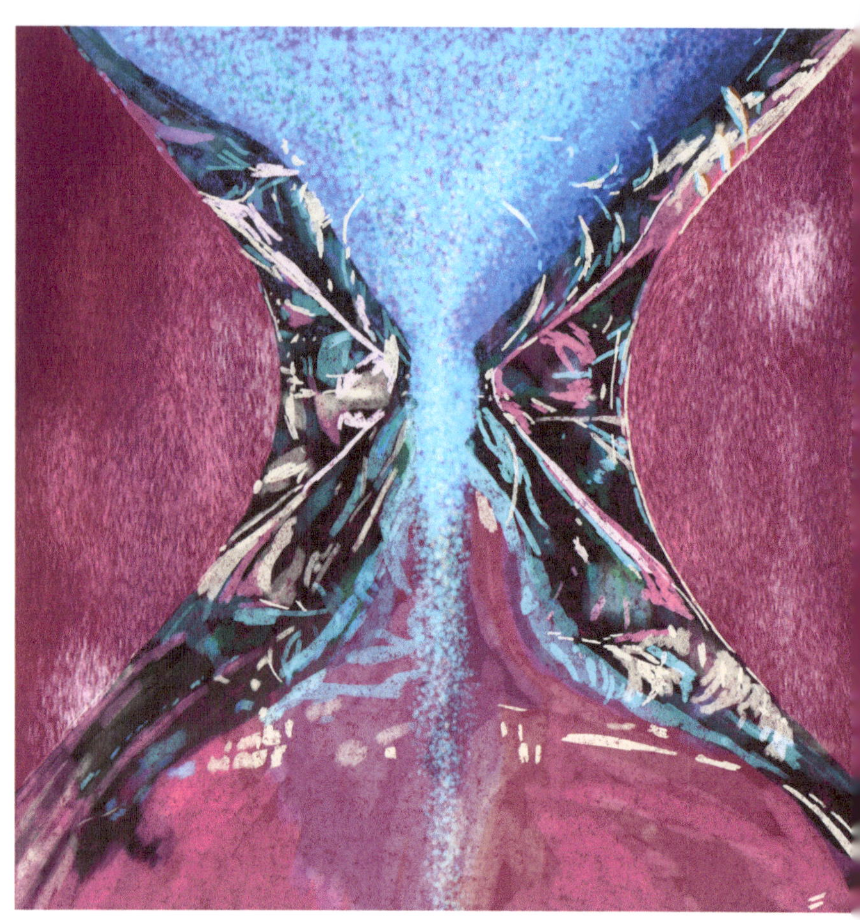

“fate”

What is time—
minutes, days, years?
Fate is unwinding
from its ageless slumber.

"kaleidoscope"

I have a
loud head and
quiet heart—
turbulent thoughts
but peaceful feelings.

The paradox
that is me
resides, not unnaturally,
in prayer and grace.

I am being led
by a holy hand
that rescued me
out of my misery.

The questions, the chaos,
pursue me.
But not knowing,
living in unknown,
grounds me
in
faith.

“present”

I am standing
on the edge.
The precipice of
anticipation
stirs restlessness
in my soul.
The past echoes
in my heart
while the future
beckons me forward.

It is hard to just be.

“overthinking”

In the morning
when I wake
I am sure.
The doubts
have not had a chance
to enter, unbidden.

It is in the evening
when the day
is at a close
that I pray
I find a way
through.

“and i am better for it”

I was young
and selfish.
I didn’t know yet
what love was.
I thought it came
nicely wrapped in a bow.

But I grew,
I wisened.
My heart began
to know
that love is selfless,
and sometimes
it lets go.

"i miss you"

The strangeness of grief,
the surprise of unshed tears,
follows the footprints
I track in the sand.

Joy is deeper
and sorrow heavier
as these years pass by,
but the grace
in loss
is the promise
of reunion.

“purpose”

Desperately—
I want
so desperately
to understand it all.
To see the threads
that have woven
my story among
this grand tapestry.

And even still
as I grapple
with my single,
burning-out match
to see—
squinting in the darkness,
hands flailing
freely about—

I know
there is purpose.

“contentment”

The first dusting of snow,
the quiet kindling of wonder,
ignites the tranquil meandering
of my soul.

Give me a hearth,
give me a blanket
and I shall be content
for hours.

“Eve was created to rule, too”

For my whole life
I thought I knew my place.
But as it turns out,
my embodiment
is not lesser than,
is not secondary,
to yours.

After all—
even God was,
and is
a ezer.

“He says i am enough”

“Not enough”
whispers a voice
in my head.

Why do you
make me feel
like I am
not enough

when Truth
tells me
I am.

“and He stoops again, and again, and again”

In the face
of eternity—
my questions, my desires,
seem small and silly.

Yet,
astounding Love stoops
to meet me
even in this space.

"He is more than enough"

When I say
I do not plan to marry,
what I mean
is that Jesus,
my savior, my anchor, my King,
is enough.
He is more than enough.
He is simply,
and extraordinarily,
more.

The gift of
my singleness,
is His sufficiency
in my life
that I have
the honor to reflect
in my unmarried status.

And when
you question my desire,
and say
"Just you wait…"
it cuts and it stings.
Because
what I hear
is "You are not enough as you are".

And while you are right,
I am not enough,
I know my Jesus is.
And with Him,
I am never alone.

"i love a good eucatastrophe"

If it were
up to me
the journey
wouldn't have known heartbreak.

But then again,
a journey with no
obstacles, surprises, or
hardship,
is hardly a journey
at all.

Part III: Becoming

"He is still giving me better things"

With stars in her eyes,
and hope in her heart,
she smiled
as God took away
her dreams,
and gave her
better things.

“thank God i am not the same”

In the waiting
I grew into myself.
The me of Then
is not the me
of Now.

I don’t hate
who I was but
I’m thankful for the grace
that did not leave me there.

“my cupboard”

The cupboard of my life
holds many jars
within its sturdy frame.

At first, only jars of love
resided on its shelves.

As time trekked on,
I accumulated more jars.

Jars of joy,
of mirth,
of grief.

And as the years added up,
some jars began to grow aged.

Now, when I open a jar of love,
it also holds remnants
of sorrow
and
hope.

"only you"

In the waiting,
You are with me.
Though my heart is heavy,
You offer peace.
Your hope is
my anchor and
Your wings, my refuge.

Mighty is Your hand,
that is just yet
offers grace.
May You always
be the treasure
of my heart and
mind and
soul.

"a dream set aside"

There are dreams
in my closet.
They are tucked away
in the disorganized boxes
of my life.

Dust coats
these square containers,
for I rarely
pull them out anymore.

But if I did,
if I found myself
glancing through those
fragile gleams of
my hopes and dreams,

I hope that
among my tears,
I would brim
with gratitude.

"give me you"

In the morning,
when I rise,
give me you—
for you are sufficient.

In the noon time,
when I think,
give me you—
for you are enough.

In the evening,
when I long,
give me you—
for you are my prize.

In the night,
when I fear,
give me you—
for you are perfect love.

“new testament family”

In the growing
she learned
that family can be found
in blood &
in Spirit.
And each was worthy
and significant
and enough.

"Your will, Your plan, not mine"

This is all
more than I expected—
more than I dreamed.

It doesn't look
how I wanted
but I
don't
mind.

Acknowledgements

Here we are again–the (somehow) hardest part of this to write.

First, thank you to my best friend, who is sitting beside me as I write this in the Poconos. Rhiannon, your friendship is a constant joy in my life—your love, support and honesty are invaluable to me. You've been there with me through all the seasons of these poems and held my (metaphorical) hand through some of the darkest days. Love you, babes!

Thank you to my sister, who has become another of my best friends. You were and are one of my favorite answers to prayer. You are the Rita to my Janet.

Thank you to my parents—you have seen every facet of who I am. Thank you for always loving and supporting me.

Thank you to Megan, Heather, and Joanna—for proofing these poems. Each one of you is a gift in my life and your friendship is a treasure.

Thank you to Kaylee and Joanna—for being my friends and for allowing me to be a part of your babies lives.

Thank you to Josh and Kristin—for not only being my coworkers but also my friends, and for being a part of the redeeming work that God was and is doing in my life.

Thank you to Ben W—your friendship has truly been a gift to me. Thank you for encouraging my creativity and always caring about me.

Thank you to Carys—how you are able to take my words and create something extraordinary is beyond me. Thank you for bringing these poems to life in such a beautiful and unique way.

And the most important thank you to my Jesus. What an honor it is to know and be known by You. To have not been left in the darkness, but to have found redemption and joy with the breaking of the dawn.

Phew. So that happened, I guess.

First, thank you for reading this far (and not only reading all of those poems, but now reading this, I suppose).

I wanted to jump back in and not only say thanks, but also explain myself a bit—after all, this is my poetry book and I can basically do what I want (sorry, not sorry).

It probably seems unrealistic, or unfinished, ending on such a high, "God is good all the time and all the time God is good" vibe in my last section. I suppose it is a bit unfinished—I am still becoming who I am meant to be. But in a way, it is finished. Because for me, I know the end. At least I know what I believe will be the end and that is my Jesus returning and making all things new, as they should be, without tears of anguish, pain or death. So I look forward to that, and the becoming of that world. I treasure this hope of that future and dwell on it often—yearning for my Redeemer's return.

I don't know you (well, maybe some of you—hi mom and dad!) but I can imagine you are somewhere on the vast spectrum that is having or relating to faith of some kind. Maybe you grew up in church, whatever denomination that might be, and you have remained in that to this day. Maybe you grew up in something, and as you grew you decided it wasn't right for you anymore and walked away (maybe even for good). Maybe you didn't grow up with a faith practice or identity and you discovered one when you were older.

Maybe you are a bit like me—growing up in an evangelical faith tradition, following all the rules to a T, but then bumped up against something that wasn't quite right, or at least didn't really fit with who Jesus said He was or called us to be. Maybe it hurt, to see something that was the foundation of your identity start to show some cracks and mold.

Maybe it caused you to feel heretical as you began questioning, hoping to be proved wrong in your suspicions or fears. Maybe you had to grieve a bit, for the faith you were raised in. And against all odds, maybe you clung tightly to the person of Jesus, knowing that regardless of what your faith tradition, your church, your very own pastor did, Jesus' word, His teachings, His love was end game.

I'm here to tell you that no matter where you are, what your journey has looked like, or where you have landed, that there is incredible hope available—that no matter the doubts, the struggles, the hurt, there is something to look forward to. Don't give up. There's more to your story, friend.

With love and gratitude,

Karalyn

Extra Poems

“creation order”

Esau was the firstborn,
yet
God chose Jacob.

Twelve brothers and
God chose Judah
in the lineage of His Son.

And David was
the youngest son but
God still made him king.

So you see–
God has a habit
of not choosing
the first.

After all,
the last
shall
be
first.

“8.8.23”

Eden.
Delight.
Perfect paradise.

The sweetest pleasure
is knowing and being known
by the singer of stars
and breather of snow.

“some of my favorite things”

Christmas music on November 1st &
sunbathing after swimming &
the first crunch of fallen leaves.

The sound of the ocean &
reading in bed &
coffee dates.

Baking cookies &
good music in the car &
candles that smell like pine trees.

Quiet time in the morning &
belly laughs &
nails painted black.

Shopping with my sister &
bosom friendships &
finding the perfect gift.

Friends who pray &
perfect movie soundtracks &
breakfast for dinner.

Children who call me auntie &
giving nicknames &
talking about Jesus.

"11.10.23"

Solomon.
Shalom.
Peace.

The wonder of it all
is found in the grace
bestowed with abandon.

"Evolution of a Future Husband"

13.
My future husband will
have green eyes and dark hair.
He will be a prince of a far away land
and he will know how to cook.

16.
My future husband will
have brown eyes and dark hair.
He will be musically talented
and he will know how to cook.

19.
My future husband will
have blue eyes and dark hair.
He will want to adopt many children
and he will know how to cook.

22.
My future husband will
have inquisitive eyes and curly, dark hair.
He will be driven to achieve
and he will know how to cook.

25.
My future husband will
have kind eyes and a generous heart.
He will seek Jesus above all else
and he will know how to cook.

28.
My future husband will
have an air of whimsy and be a notion of the past.
He will be a dream, wonderfully set aside.

And *I* know how to cook.

About the Author

Karalyn lives in NEPA with her mountains of books and dreams of one day running away to a small cottage by the sea. *With Stars In Her Eyes* is her second collection of poetry.

You can contact her at: *karalynelysepoetry@gmail.com.*

About the Illustrator

Carys is somehow an accountant with a Bachelors of Science in counseling from Clarks Summit University. She lives in NEPA with a completely reasonable amount of plants. Carys has always loved drawing and imaginging about other worlds. This is her first published collection of illustrations.

About the Publisher

Started by two brothers, *The Nights & Weekends* is a creative collective focused on bringing artists together to collaborate and encourage one another in their work.

www.ingramcontent.com/pod-product-compliance
Ingram Content Group UK Ltd.
Pitfield, Milton Keynes, MK11 3LW, UK
UKHW061026310726
14090UKWH00024B/420

* 9 7 9 8 9 9 5 7 1 5 6 0 3 *